HOW TO LOOK AFTER YOUR PET

PUPPY

Mark Evans

B.Vet.Med.

DK

DORLING KINDERSLEY

**LONDON, NEW YORK, MUNICH, PARIS,
MELBOURNE AND DELHI**

DK

A DORLING KINDERSLEY BOOK
www.dk.com

For Bubble!

Project Editor Liza Bruml
Art Editor Jane Coney
Editor Miriam Farbey
Designer Rebecca Johns
Photographer Steve Shott
Illustrator Sally Hynard

Published in Great Britain by
Dorling Kindersley Limited
A Penguin Company
80 Strand, London, WC2R 0RL

6 8 10 9 7 5

A CIP catalogue record for this book
is available from the British Library.

ISBN 0-7513-5397-3

Colour reproduction by Colourscan, Singapore
Printed and bound in Spain by Artes Gráficas Toledo, S.A.
D.L. TO: 148-2002

Models: Robin Bloomfield, Jacob Brubert, Sophie Bunten,
Martin Cooles, Laura Douglas, Georgina Drake, Darius Jones,
Emma Jones, Paul Mitchell, Serena Palmer, Florence Prowen,
Isabel Prowen, Lauren Stewart, Maia Terry

Dorling Kindersley would like to thank everyone who
allowed us to photograph their pet, Wood Green Animal
Shelters for providing dogs, Christopher Howson for
design help, Bridget Hopkinson for editorial help and
Lynn Bresler for the index.

Picture credits: Paul Bricknell p20 tr, p23 bl, p25 tr, front
cover c, back cover c; Dave King p13 br, p18 tc, tr, cr, cl, bl,
br, p19 cl, bc, br; Jerry Young p12 tr, tl, p14 tl, p16 tl

Note to parents
This book teaches your child how to be
a caring and responsible pet owner. But
remember, your child must have your help
and guidance in every aspect of day-to-day
pet care. Don't let your child have a dog
unless you are sure that your family has
the time and resources to look after it·
properly – for the whole of its life.

Contents

Introduction

The first step to becoming a good dog owner is to choose the right sort of dog. It is how a dog behaves that is most important, not what she looks like or how old she is. She is going to be your best friend. You'll spend a lot of time playing together. But remember, you need to look after her every day. Not just to start with, but for the whole of her life.

Shopping basket full of things you will need

Understanding your pet
By watching how your dog behaves, you will learn her special way of talking to you. Your dog also watches every move you make. She likes to see a smile on your face, so she will learn quickly to do things that please you.

Your dog does a play-bow to invite you to play

Caring for your pet
You will only be your dog's best friend if you care for her properly. You will need to make sure that she eats the right foods, always has water, and gets plenty of exercise every day. You will also have to groom her regularly, and spend time training her.

You will have to groom every part of your dog

Out and about

There are lots of things you can do with your dog. She is better at some games than you are! If you keep her under control, and clean up after her, you will show everyone you are a good dog owner.

You will need to visit your vet centre regularly

Your dog will need plenty of exercise

People to help

The best dog owner always tries to find out more about her dog. You can ask your vet and nurse how to keep your pet healthy and happy.

New family member

Your dog will be a part of your family. She can even make a good friend for some of your other pets. But you will have to train her to obey the rules you and your family make for her.

Ask a grown-up

👫 When you see this sign, you should ask an adult to help you.

Your dog will become part of your family

Things to remember

When you live with a pet dog, there are some important rules you must always follow:

🐾 Wash your hands after stroking or playing with your dog.

🐾 Don't let your dog lick your face.

🐾 Never allow your dog to eat food from your plate.

🐾 Don't let your dog on your bed.

🐾 If your dog is fast asleep, don't wake her up suddenly.

🐾 Always put on your dog's collar and lead before you take her out.

🐾 Don't take your dog into a shop that sells food.

🐾 Never, ever hit your dog.

What is a dog?

Dogs belong to a group of animals called mammals. Like all mammals, dogs have warm blood and a hairy body. When young, they drink milk from their mothers. Not all dogs look the same. They may be big or small, short-haired or long-haired. As they grow up, they develop keen senses and four strong legs on which to run.

Ear turns to pick up sounds from every direction

Mouth is strong enough to bite through metal

Tongue out as she pants to keep cool

Thick skin keeps her warm

Dogs usually have ten nipples

Eye open even while she rests

Flat tummy button is covered with hair

Rough toe pads give good grip

Underneath your dog
Look closely and you will find that your dog has a tummy button just like you. Count the nipples. You should find ten. In mother dogs, they are sucked for milk by her young puppies.

Life on four legs
Every part of your dog's body does its own job. Strong muscles power her so she can run and run. Her four legs keep her steady and her hairy coat helps to keep her warm. She uses her tail for balance and to signal her mood to the rest of her pack.

Alert dog has
perked-up ears

Third eyelid
keeps eye clean

Cold, wet
nose picks up
the faintest
smells

Tongue licks to
feel – just like
you use your fingers

Super senses
Your dog has keener senses
than you. She can sniff you
coming before you've walked
through the door. She perks
her ears up to listen when you
think it's quiet. She can see
farther behind her than you,
and more clearly in dim light.

Look closer at your dog

The pointy teeth
are called canines

Whiskers are used
to feel when it's too
dark to see

Hair drops out, or
moults, when it
grows long

Thick coat keeps
her warm

Nails are good
for digging

Wagging tail
means your
dog is happy

Oily fur is
like a raincoat

She always stands
on tiptoe

Spongy pads
protect the fine
toe bones

Life in the wild

Dogs are members of a family of animals called canids. Wild members of the canid family include the wolf, the dingo, the red fox and the coyote. Most canids live with other members of their family in a pack. A few thousand years ago, people began to look after friendly wolves. They cared for the babies of the tamest. The wolves and their offspring soon became man's best friend – the dog.

European wolf

From wild to tame

It may seem amazing, but it is very likely that a wolf is the ancestor of your dog. They both like to scavenge and hunt. And they both like living together in a pack, rather than being alone.

Pack life

Today, some people keep hound dogs in packs for hunting. Each pack, like this pack of Beagles, contains dogs of all ages from puppies to wise grandparents. There's a real team spirit in the pack, with everyone looking after each other.

Old dog lets the younger dogs go first

Shy dog feels safe in middle of pack

Tail is held high

Bold dog keeps a sharp lookout

12

Order in the pack

Just like a football team, the dog pack is led by a captain, and has different positions and rules. One dog, usually a male, is the leader. He is helped by a female. Together, they boss the other dogs, making sure that rules are kept. All the other dogs have a place in the pack. Each one knows which dog to obey, and which one to boss around.

Parents are pack leaders

Children rank second

Dog lies at the feet of her masters

Top female dog waits for orders from the leader

The new family pack

When you get a dog, you and your family become her pack. You and your parents need to decide the rules for your dog. As long as she understands them, she will be happy to be looked after.

The Mastiff – the biggest and bravest dog

The pack leader is always alert

Young dog sniffs the ground for scent trails

The first breeds

The first people to keep dogs as pets found that not all their dogs were the same. Some were faster than others, some were braver and some were better hunters. By choosing which mother and father dog had puppies, early pet owners bred different kinds of dogs.

All shapes and sizes

Think of the grown-ups that you know. Most of them are probably about the same shape and size. But that is not true of adult dogs. Some are so small you can carry them under one arm, while others are so big you can't get both your arms around them for a hug! What they have in common is that they are all made in the same way and need the same things.

Purebreds and mongrels

Dogs that look alike belong to the same breed. But many dogs are mixed breeds, called mongrels. No two mongrels look the same. They often have the best parts of two dogs rolled into one.

Tail held high

One ear may flop forward

Droopy ears are as soft as velvet

Coat marked with a saddle of darker fur

Long and fluffy fur

Small friend
A tiny breed from China, the Pekingese was often carried in his proud owner's coat sleeve.

Energy for life
A Jack Russell Terrier never seems to get tired. He needs lots of exercise and enjoys being out and about.

Little legs
The Basset Hound got his name from the French word "bas", meaning "low", because his tummy is so near the ground.

Adorable bundle of fun

Think ahead before you fall for a fluffy puppy. It is easy to pick up and cuddle a young St Bernard puppy, but he will soon grow to be one of the biggest dogs in the world.

St Bernard puppy

St Bernard dog

How big will he grow?

The size of a puppy's mother and father will give you an idea of how big he will get. The size of the puppy's paws are another clue. If the puppy looks as if he's got very large paws, then he may well grow into a big dog.

Puppy's mother is big and tall

An eye patch like a pirate's

Long, droopy tail

Short and sleek coat

Face is friendly

Chest puffed out proudly

Fur is long and shaggy

Legs are thin but strong

Every one is different

Mongrel dogs come in all shapes and sizes. They are probably the most common dogs in the world.

Built like a boxer

The Boxer must be well trained as she is very strong. Like other big dogs, she can easily knock you over.

Huge and idle

The Irish Wolfhound needs a lot of space to live in but does not need nearly as much exercise as you might think.

Breeds and behaviour

Find out as much as you can about different types or breeds of dog. Some types of dog need plenty of exercise while others are lazy. Some types of dog make good guard dogs while others will be keen to join in and play with you and your friends. You want a dog that will fit in happily with you, your family and your home.

Yorkshire Terrier

Toy Poodle

❧ Choosing a male or a female
Very young male and female puppies are quite similar. But as male puppies grow older, they can become stubborn. They may even wander away from home, looking for girlfriends! Female dogs, called bitches, can be easier to look after.

Chatterboxes
Some dogs have a lot to say for themselves. They can go on barking and yapping for hours without a break! Oddly enough, the smallest dogs are often the noisiest.

Family dogs
Many mongrel dogs and some breed dogs are happy and friendly. They enjoy playing games and being cuddled. You can take them with you anywhere and they'll always be good.

Labrador

Mongrel

Cavalier King Charles Spaniel

English Springer
Spaniel

Trainable dogs

Several kinds of dog like to use their brains more than others. They need to have something to do all the time or they will get bored. These dogs are easy to train. They like a real challenge, such as a hurdle (see p38).

Border
Collie

Mongrel

German
Shepherd

Good guard dogs

Little or large, some dogs are not always friendly. They don't like to be told what to do by strangers and they can be difficult to make friends with. Many of them are not really suitable for a busy family, but they do make very good guard dogs.

Dachshunds

Athlete or dawdler

Not all big dogs need to have lots of exercise. In fact, some are quite lazy. On the other hand, many small dogs need plenty of exercise. You must have the time to take them for long walks.

Hold on firmly as puppy is racing away

Athletic
Whippet

Lazy
Great Dane

17

Selecting for looks

All dogs have the same parts – a head with eyes, ears, mouth and nose, and a body with a furry coat. The size, shape and colour of these parts is different in each dog. But don't be tempted to choose a dog just for his looks. Look at the way that he behaves as well. After all, you are choosing a friend for life.

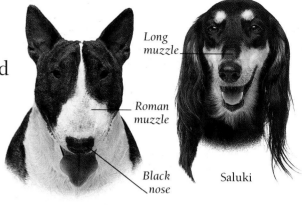

Long muzzle

Roman muzzle

Black nose

Bull Terrier

Saluki

Nice noses
All dogs' noses are cold and wet. But the muzzle, which attaches the nose to a dog's head, varies in shape and size.

Flat muzzle

Pug

Pointed, furry ears

Papillon

Bloodhound

Long and droopy ear

Prick ear

Flap ear

Jack Russell Terrier

Coat colours
A dog's coat can be black, brown, red, yellow or white, or a mixture of any of these colours.

Black and brown Airedale Terrier

Droopy or perked ears?
Dogs can have all kinds of ears. They may be covered with long hair or they may be quite smooth. Some dogs have small, pointed ears while others have long, floppy ones.

West Highland White Terrier

Multi-coloured Cavalier King Charles Spaniel

atches and spots

dog's coat can have amazing
arkings. Some dogs just have
ne large patch. Others are
overed in so many spots you
an't count them all!

Black patch over one eye

Lots of black spots

The rest of the coat is white

Mongrel with a patch

Spotty Dalmatian

From purebred dog to mongrel

Two purebreds have another purebred

Purebred looks the same as its parents

Different purebreds have a crossbred

A crossbred is a mixture of its parents

Two crossbreds have a mongrel

Every mongrel dog looks different

Coat patterns

Many dogs have patterned coats. Brindle
pattern is a streaky brown and black. Merle
is a blotchy pattern of black, white and
grey. Mongrel dogs can have
coats of all different patterns.

Brown and black brindle pattern

Mixed coat pattern

Merle pattern

Boxer

Mongrel

Corgi

airstyles for dogs

ogs can have as many different
airstyles as people. They can
ave short hair, long
air, silky hair, wiry
air or curly hair.

Schnauzer

Wiry hair

Afghan Hound

Long coat is silky

Mongrel

Short coat is smooth

Where to find your new puppy

You can get your new pet from a friend, a dog breeder or an animal shelter. The nurse at your vet centre will give you names and addresses of breeders and shelters. The nurse will also help you make a list of the things you need. Make sure that you have got them all ready before you go to fetch your dog.

Puppy tears up slipper with his teeth

The trouble-maker
Before you fall for an adorable puppy, think carefully. A puppy is often a lot of trouble. He may scratch the furniture and chew your favourite slippers.

Older and wiser
If you don't have time to keep an eye on a puppy, get a dog. He should already be toilet trained and so should be easier to look after.

Well-behaved dog sits quietly

The animal shelter
You can find both puppies and older dogs at an animal shelter. Get to know a dog before making a choice.

Try taking the dog you like for a walk

Proud mother lets puppies drink

Golden Labrador

This puppy will be for sale when he is six weeks old

Buying a purebred
Purebred dogs are very expensive. You can buy a breed dog from a breeder. Breeders allow their purebred dogs to have puppies.

Collar

Buy a strong nylon dog collar. Attach a disc engraved with your dog's name, and your address and telephone number.

Identity disc

Nylon collar

Bowl has wide rim to keep it steady

Water bowl

Food bowl

Dinner things

Buy two different coloured plastic bowls, one for food and another for water. Choose a spoon and a fork that you will only use for your dog's food.

Spoon

Fork

Squeaky clean

Your puppy will often make a mess. You will need some special cleaning things to clean up after it.

Odour remover

Towel   Rubber gloves   Disinfectant

Carrying box

You will need a carrying box to take your puppy home in.

Toy bone

Toy ring

Rubber toys

Puppies love to chew things. You can buy rubber toys in different shapes and colours.

Resting box

A cut-up cardboard box makes a warm and cosy place for your puppy to rest in.

Naming your puppy

Think of a name for your puppy. The best names are short ones, like Jet or Tess. Have the name engraved on your puppy's identity disc.

Danger!
Some things can hurt dogs.

Sharp scissors may cut your dog

Trailing electric cables might be chewed

Rubbish may choke your puppy

Hot drinks will scald a dog's skin

Cleaning fluids are poisonous

Eating plants may make your dog ill

An open gate will let a puppy get out

A puppy can drown even in shallow water

21

Choosing a healthy puppy

It is a good idea to first look at a litter of puppies when they are four weeks old. But you won't be able to take one home until it is at least six weeks old. When you choose a puppy, be sure to meet the mother dog. Look for a puppy that is friendly and healthy.

1 Talk to the puppy's mother. Make sure she is the kind of dog you would like your puppy to grow into. Sometimes you may be lucky enough to meet the father.

Friendly mother tries to lick you to say hello

Tail wags – mother's glad to see her puppies

Mother keeps a lookout

Legs apart to let puppies suckle

2 When the owner takes you and the mother dog to the puppies, try to watch from a place where the puppies can't see you. The strongest puppy will push to the front to suck milk from his mother's nipples.

3 After a few minutes, sit down with the puppies. They will think you are a great big dog and climb all over you. Don't touch them. Look for a lively puppy that likes playing with his brothers and sisters, but is not a bully.

This puppy isn't interested

Happy puppy wags tail

Shy puppy

Friendly puppy

Alert puppy

Curious puppy

Be careful not to tread on a puppy

4 **Gently stroke** the puppy that you like the most to see if he is friendly. Ask the owner the sex of the puppy. Also check that the puppy hasn't been chosen by someone else.

Stroke the puppy's head carefully

A healthy puppy should smell milky

Paperwork
Write down the type of food your puppy eats and the names of medicines and injections he has been given. Your vet will want to know. If your puppy is a purebred, don't forget to ask for his papers.

5 **Ask the owner** how to pick up the puppy. Then check that he is healthy. He should have clear eyes. His nose should be cold and wet. His coat should be clean, even under his tail.

Cold, wet nose   *Clean ears*   *Fluffy coat*

Holes let in air so puppy can breathe

6 **Go back to collect** your puppy when he is at least six weeks old. Take with you a collar and name tag to fasten round his neck. Also bring a carrying box to keep your new puppy in on the journey home.

Two fingers should fit under collar so puppy can breathe

Welcome home

Remember your first day at school. You were scared without your parents, but you soon made new friends. Your puppy may be frightened when she leaves her mother. To help her settle in quickly, get everything ready before you go to fetch her.

Nose up to sniff new smells

Visiting your vet

You should arrange to visit your vet on the way home from collecting your new puppy. The vet will examine your pet all over to make sure she is healthy. He will also tell you if she needs any medicines (see p45).

What sex is your puppy?

When a puppy is very young, it can be hard to tell whether it is a male or a female. Ask your vet to check the sex.

Hold on tight

You may want to pick up your puppy to cuddle her or to stop her getting into trouble! Put one arm behind her front legs and the other under her bottom. If she keeps wriggling, gently put her down.

Keep her close to your chest

Ticking lulls puppy to sleep, like her mother's heartbeat

Your puppy may be heavy, so hold on firmly

Leave a bowl of fresh water

The food bowl should always be left clean

Worried stare at
the new puppy

Meeting the family
Your puppy and your cat may become best friends. Watch them carefully to make sure they don't fight.

Sniffing the
new friend

Crouching ready to
make a quick getaway

Cosy corner
When you can watch over your new puppy, she can rest in her box. Put the box in a warm, quiet place. At bedtime, and when you can't be with her, put her in her special puppy crate (see p30).

Put hot water bottle
under white, furry rug

Hot water bottle comforts
puppy as it is warm like
her brothers and sisters

Strong box has
front cut out

Soft, furry rug is
nice to curl up on

Strong rubber toy
is safe to leave
for your puppy

Put a layer of old paper
under the box and bowls
to keep the floor clean

Change the paper as
soon as it gets dirty

Feeding your puppy

Your puppy will eat meat and vegetables, but what she finds tasty is not always good for her. To keep your puppy fit, it is best to buy food specially made for dogs. Make sure the food you buy is correct for your puppy. You can choose between moist and dry food. Ask your vet to help you choose the right food for your dog.

"Complete" dry food

"Complete" dry food with water added

"Complete" moist food

All-in-one
The simplest way to feed your puppy is with a "complete" food. It contains everything she needs. The food is either wet or dry. Dry food is good for your puppy's teeth because it needs a lot of chewing.

"Complementary" food

Half and half
Some foods, called "complementary", must be mixed with other foods to make a healthy meal.

"Complementary" moist food

Dry mixer biscuit

Look for the word "dog"

"Complete" food needs nothing added

Feeding guide tells you how much to feed

DOG FOOD

Fully tested

Food is for dogs over one year old. It is a complete pet food.

Feed straight from the packet
Suggested daily amounts:
Small – Corgi 100 to 150 grams
Medium – Spaniel 150 to 250 grams
Large – Labrador 250 to 400 grams

Ingredients: meat, vegetables
Protein ~%, Oil ~%, Fibre ~%,
Water ~%, Vitamins A, D, E
Always leave fresh water

Best before

grams

Look for the word "tested"

Recycling sign

Use by date

Weight

Bar code

Buying the food
Carefully read the writing on the packet. Make sure the food is for dogs, not cats. Check the food is suitable for your dog. This label is from a food for grown-up dogs. A puppy needs a food for growing dogs. Look and see if you need to add anything to the food.

Fresh water daily

Always make sure your puppy has a bowl of clean water. Without it, she will quickly become ill. Never give her milk, fruit juice or soft drink.

Sturdy water bowl

Measure the food carefully

Use a special spoon

Milk can make your dog sick

Bone-shaped snacks

Chewy treats

Your leftovers may upset your dog's tummy

How much to feed

The label will tell you how much to feed your puppy every day. You may need to know how heavy she is. If your puppy gets chubby, give her less food. If you start to see her bones, you should ask your vet for help.

Time for a treat

Just as most of us love eating sweets, your puppy will wolf down any dog treats you give to her. She doesn't know that too many are bad for her. Give her a special treat when she is good, but not when she asks for one.

Chocolate will make your dog fat

Bones may choke your dog

Feeding times

Give your puppy small meals three or four times a day. When she is older, she will only need two meals a day. Feed her just after your breakfast and evening meal.

Too many treats will spoil your dog

Leave food down for no more than 20 minutes

Puppy waits patiently for her meal

Put the bowl in a quiet corner

Understanding your dog

Your dog doesn't talk to you by saying words. Instead, she uses parts of her body to tell you what she is thinking. Just as you smile when you are happy, she shows her mood by changing the look on her face, the way she stands and the position of her ears and tail. If you watch her carefully, you will soon understand what she is trying to say.

Eyes plead

Sitting upright

Paw is held out

The beggar

When your dog was a tiny puppy, she held up a paw to ask for food from her mother. Now she is older, begging can be for anything. She may want food or to go for a walk. But don't always give in!

Make sure you look cross

Speak in a firm voice

Hang-dog

If your dog lies down and puts her ears back, you know that she has understood you are telling her off. She looks sad because she knows that you are upset with her.

Point straight at your dog

Head held high to bark

Tail wags

Eyes look up timidly

Ears fold flat

Stand up tall and straight

Barks, howls and growls

Your dog makes noises. She barks to warn you if someone is outside. She howls when she is lonely and growls when she is angry. She whines if she wants your attention.

Body crouched in shame

Alert ears

Eyes glare without blinking

Fur on neck stands up

Tail upright

Leave me alone!
When your dog gets angry, she looks threatening. Her hair stands on end and her tail is held straight so she looks big and frightening. She curls up her lip and growls.

Happy puppy tries to get very close to you

Tail flies from side to side

Curly tail

Stretched back

Bent on front legs

The play-bow
Your dog tells you when she wants to play a game by crouching on her front legs with her bottom in the air. This is called a play-bow. She wags her tail and drums her front legs on the floor.

Pleased to see you
Your dog shows you when she is happy. Her tail wags so hard that you may think it's going to fall off! She will try to lick your face – don't let her.

Hind leg raised

Tummy is a favourite tickling spot

Head back

Paws in the air
Sometimes your dog rolls over on his back. He is saying that you are his boss and are allowed to stroke his tummy.

Toilet training your puppy

Toilet training is teaching your puppy where she is allowed to go to the toilet. The best way to toilet train your puppy is to use a special puppy crate. As she learns not to make a mess indoors, you must teach her where to go to the toilet outdoors.

🐾 The puppy crate

A puppy crate is a special room for your puppy. She will never make a mess in her own room unless it is too big. Then she will sleep in one end and use the other end as her toilet.

At night, put a towel over the crate

A clean bedroom

At night, and when you can't watch your puppy, put her in the crate. When you let her out of the crate, take her outside for a toilet trip straight away. If she wakes up at night, you will also have to take her to the toilet.

Puppy feels safe in the crate

Line the crate with a fleece rug

Your puppy's favourite toy

Same place, same time
Pick a place in the garden for your puppy's toilet. Take her to the same place every time. She will need to go to the toilet after she has eaten and when she wakes up.

Female dog squats   Male dog cocks leg

Cocking a leg
Very young male and female puppies look the same when they go to the toilet. They both squat. As a male grows older, he begins to lift one leg when he urinates.

Puppy sniffs the ground – time to take her out

Walking in circles

Female puppy squats when she goes to the toilet

Giving the command
Your puppy needs to learn to go when you tell her to. Keep telling her to go, saying a special word like "Pooh" and wait. It may take a few minutes for your puppy to go, but don't give up.

The best reward
Cuddle and praise your puppy when she has finished. Then clean up any mess with your pooper-scooper.

Stroke puppy to reward her

Wash your hands afterwards

Odour remover takes away the smell

Disinfectant kills germs

Wear gloves

Accidents will happen
All young puppies have accidents indoors. When this happens, you must clean the mess up properly. If your puppy can still smell it, she will probably have another accident in the same spot.

Training your dog

Train your dog to remember those things you want him to do, such as to sit, stay or fetch the newspaper. Dogs learn in a very simple way. If it's fun, it must be worth doing again! Start to train your dog as soon as you get him but keep the lessons short. Try a one-minute training session lots of times a day, and your friends won't believe their eyes when they see what you both can do.

1 Teaching your dog to sit is easy. Each time he sits down, say the word "Sit" slowly and clearly. Soon he will learn to sit each time that you tell him to.

2 Now train your dog to stay when you walk away. Put your hand out flat towards your dog's face. Say "Stay" slowly. Then gradually take a few steps back, repeating "Stay". If your dog follows you, begin again.

Look at your dog

Say "Come" and call his name

Beckon him with your arms

Stretch out your arm

Stand up straight

Puppy waits patiently

Watch his tail wagging as he rushes towards you

3 Next teach your dog to come to you when you call. Use a long lead until you are sure he will not run off. Bend down so he can see your eyes and wait a moment. Then call him, using his name and the word "Come".

4 **Your dog should sit** at your feet when he comes to you. Make sure he doesn't jump up. A puppy leaping up to your face may be fun, but when he grows bigger, he could knock you over.

Naughty puppy!
A puppy is always getting into trouble. She thinks that tearing up a cushion is an exciting game.

Don't look at your puppy

Don't touch your puppy

5 Praise your dog straight away whenever he does as he is asked. He does not have a long memory and soon forgets what he has just done. One of the best rewards is a plain old hug!

Kneel down to stroke your dog

A fair punishment
If you catch your puppy being naughty, simply say "No" and your dog's name in a firm voice. Do not play with her. Your puppy will look sad, but don't give in.

Puppy tries to say hello

The last resort
If your puppy continues to misbehave, keep saying "No" patiently. You can put her in her crate for a short time. Never, ever hit your puppy.

How to reward an obedient dog
❖ Give your dog a big cuddle to show him that he's part of your family.
❖ Take your dog for a walk – he loves to be out and about.
❖ Let him play with his favourite toy.
❖ Give him a food treat, but don't spoil him with special food too often.

Out and about

 All dogs need exercise to keep them fit. Take your dog for a walk every day. You must always keep him under control, especially near busy roads. Not everyone likes dogs as much as you do. Walk to an area with lots of space where you and your dog are allowed to play.

Collar with name tag

Harness

Head-collar

Extension lead

Lead

Keeping control
Fasten a collar and lead round your dog so he can't run away. Put a chest harness on a small dog. A muzzle that fits over the head and neck will help you control a very big dog.

Bag with pooper-scooper and towel

Side by side
Train your dog to walk by your side. When he tries to pull ahead, say "Heel". If he still tugs, tell him to sit. Only walk on when he is calm.

Toy to play with

Dog walks calmly by your side

Finding friends
When you are out walking, you will meet other dogs. Your dog will sniff the stranger to find out if it is a male or a female. The smell also tells him if the dog is friendly.

Looking closely at the stranger

Strange dog sniffs your dog

Time to play!
Your dog wants to join in your games. He likes throwing and catching the best. He will jump up to try and catch what you throw. If he misses, he will pick it up from the ground in his mouth and bring it back to you.

Dog barks very excitedly

Tail curls upwards

Dog jumps high to catch

Balancing on back legs

Balancing on front leg

Outdoor dangers

Strange dogs may frighten your young puppy

Rubbish may get caught in your dog's throat

Your dog must not worry sheep

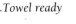

It is not safe for dogs to swim in deep water

Keep your dog away from traffic

Keeping clean
Your dog may go to the toilet on your walk. Help keep your neighbourhood tidy. Scoop up everything with your pooper-scooper.

Scooping up with the pooper-scooper

Stand well back or you will be soaked

Towel ready

Dog shakes from side to side

Wrap towel around dog

All dry again
If your dog is damp, he may get cold. Rub him dry all over with his towel.

Shaking dry
Your dog will splash through puddles. He loves to go paddling. Make sure he shakes off the water while you are still outside.

Good grooming

Your dog is covered in fur from her nose to the tip of her tail. This hairy coat helps to keep her warm. The oil in it stops her skin from getting wet. It's like your jumper and your raincoat, all in one! Groom your dog's fur every day to keep it clean and shiny.

Rubber grooming glove

Wire comb

Grooming brush

Grooming tools
Buy your dog a grooming brush and a wire comb with rounded prongs. If your dog has short fur, you just need a special rubber glove.

Teeth pull dirt from hair

Licked clean
Your dog can reach to clean most parts of her body. She uses her front teeth as a comb and her rough tongue as a flannel.

Stroke her gently

1 **Before you start** to groom your dog, talk to her. If you tell her what you're going to do, she will be more relaxed.

Grooming comb

Wire bristles

Soft bristles

Brush her fur downward

2 **Start by brushing** your dog's back. Use the wire-bristle side of the brush. Pull it through her coat from her neck to her tail. If you find any knots, untangle them with your fingers. Then brush her back again with the soft-bristle side.

3 Then comb your dog's legs, tail, neck, tummy and ears. Be careful not to tickle her. Groom each part in the same order every day. If you remember the order you won't miss anything!

Comb ears down from her head

Long hair on feet tangles easily

4 Groom her back again. She likes this best. If she is restless when you comb her ears, she will stay if she remembers that her back will be brushed in the end.

Soft bristles make her coat shine

Dog sits patiently while back is groomed

5 Praise your dog for being patient by giving her a big cuddle. If you always reward her (see p33), she will be happy to be groomed every day.

Brushed coat is sleek

Grooming a short-haired dog

If your dog has a very short coat, give her a good rub every day with a grooming glove. The small rubber bumps take away old hairs, dust and dirt.

Stroke fur with glove

37

Your puppy grows up

You will have to look after your young puppy just like his mother did. But by the time he is a year old, he is grown up. He loves to be out and about. He likes to do things with you and he sees you as his best friend. After many years, your dog will grow old. Then he will need special care to keep him healthy.

Caring for a puppy
A young puppy is helpless. He needs his mother to give him food and to clean up after him all day, every day. When he is old enough to leave his mother, you must look after him just like she did.

The high jump
When your dog is fully grown, you can do lots of exciting things together. To clear a hurdle you need to work as a team. You and your dog have to run and jump at the same time, or the hurdle may fall over.

Tail up for balance

Right leg bent up behind to avoid hurdle

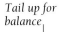

Back legs fly over hurdle

Left leg out for landing

Hurdle does not fall

Front legs out for landing

Things to do with your dog
❉ Join a local dog club.
❉ Enter competitions for the best-trained dog.
❉ Compete in dog relay races.
❉ Go on sponsored walks.
❉ Cross-country running.

Shining black ears

Rosette for the winning owner

Groomed coat

Prize-winning dog

Showing your dog

You can take your dog to a dog show. The judge will give prizes to the dogs that are the best examples of their type or breed.

Old dog lies quietly

Plastic, oval dog bed

Soft fleece

Caring for an elderly dog

Even when your dog is older, she will love to play. She may be slower, so don't wear her out. Do not disturb her when she is asleep. Make sure she eats the right food (see p26). Take her to your vet regularly for a check-up.

Leaving your dog

Leaving for a short time

When you first get your dog, he may howl when you leave him. Don't pay any attention, or he will think that you will come back every time he howls. You should never leave your dog alone for more than four hours.

Going on holiday

You can't always take your dog with you when you go on holiday. You can put him in kennels, which is like a hotel for dogs. Take his favourite toys so he doesn't feel homesick. Remember to leave a note saying what you feed him, and the name and telephone number of your vet.

Staying with friends

You may be lucky enough to have friends to look after your dog. But remember, dog-sitting is more than taking a dog to the toilet twice a day. Your dog needs to be fed at the right times and taken for walks. Make a list that explains how to look after your dog.

In the car

Most dogs like to travel in the car. You must make sure that your dog is secure – put him in his crate or buy a special dog seat belt. Don't let him put his head out of the window. Never, ever leave your dog in the car in hot weather. Even with a window open, he will get too hot.

Neutering your puppy

Just as grown-up women can have children, a female dog can have puppies. You should think very carefully about whether you want your dog to have puppies. Your vet can give male and female dogs an operation, called neutering, when they are six months old. After it, a female dog cannot be a mother, and a male dog cannot be a father.

The same but different
Your dog looks almost the same after a neutering operation as he or she did before it. But your dog will act differently. A neutered male dog does not try to look for a girlfriend. A neutered female dog does not worry about having a litter of puppies.

❋ **Responsible owner**
You may think it is fun for your female dog to have puppies. But it is usually best to have your dog neutered. Letting a dog have puppies can be very expensive. You need to do a lot of planning and you have to find good homes for all of the puppies.

You won't feel any difference

1 Puppies are born with their eyes closed, and they can't hear. They smell their mother, and crawl to her for a drink of milk. Their mother licks them to keep them clean.

Mother keeps a close watch

Puppy pushes to try to drink milk from a nipple

This puppy feels left out

*Young puppy
licks his brother*

2 **At five weeks old**, the puppies are much larger. They spend most of their time playing with their brothers and sisters. They race around, although they are still wobbly and sometimes fall over. They will soon be ready to leave their mother.

*Puppy sniffs the
ground curiously*

3 **A sixteen-week-old puppy** thinks like a teenage person. As the puppy has left her mother, you are now her best friend. She is very clever. You must spend lots of time training her to make sure that she doesn't get into too much mischief.

*Cuddle your puppy
to comfort her*

*Puppy sits
happily with her
new "mother"*

*Puppy is
now a fully
grown dog*

4 **After about a year**, your puppy has become a grown-up dog. If she wasn't neutered at six months old, she is ready to have puppies. If her brothers weren't neutered, they are old enough to be fathers.

Health care

You need to look after your dog properly to make sure that she stays healthy. You should feed her the right food (see p26), keep her well groomed (p36), and take her for walks regularly (p34). You also need to do some quick and simple health checks. If you do these every day, you will learn to spot quickly if your dog is unwell.

Push the fur back to see the skin

1 **Check that your dog's coat** is in good condition. Run your fingers through her fur. It should feel soft and silky, and smell clean. Don't forget to check the hidden places, like under the tail.

2 **Tell your dog to lie down** so you can look at her nails and paws. Look between her toes and at her pads to check there are no splinters.

Nail is the right length

Nail is too long

Hold puppy so she can't wriggle away

One hand pulls on forehead

Put one hand under muzzle

Check nothing is stuck in the hair between the pads

Examine each paw in turn

3 **Look at each of your dog's eyes.** A bright light will help you see them better. Each eye should be clear and shiny, with no tears in the corner.

4 Make sure that nothing is stuck in your dog's mouth. Hold her muzzle in one hand and her jaw in the other. Pull your hands apart slowly to open her mouth.

Check nothing is between the teeth

Watch out for your fingers

Pull ear flap back

5 Examine your dog's ears. Hold back the flappy part of each ear in turn and look down the hairy hole. The ear should be clean. If it smells, your dog may be ill.

Puppy chews on toy

Toy has grooves for toothpaste

Pearly white teeth
Your vet will show you chews and toys that help keep your dog's teeth clean.

Teeth-cleaning toy

Toothbrush

Dog toothpaste

6 Brush your dog's teeth every day. Put some dog toothpaste on your dog's toothbrush and put the brush in her mouth. Brush in and out along the outsides of her teeth.

Puppy tries to chew the brush

Your pet care check list
Use this list to keep a record of all the jobs you need to do.

Copy this chart. Tick off the jobs when you have finished them.

Every day:
Feed your dog
Clean food bowls
Put down fresh water
Walk your dog
Practise training
Groom coat
Check fur
Examine paws
Check ears and eyes
Look inside mouth
Clean teeth

◆

Once a week:
Weigh your dog
Clean collar and lead
Check food supplies

◆

Every month:
Give medicines
Wash fur blanket

◆

Every year:
Take your dog to the vet for a check-up
Injections

Visiting your vet centre

The vets and the nurses who work at your local vet centre want to help you keep your dog healthy and happy. They will tell you how to look after your dog properly. You can ask them as many questions as you like. They will also try to make your dog better if she is ill.

Bandage

Large bandage

Cotton wool

Tape

Salt sachets

Scissors   Dressing   Disinfectant   Muzzle

Strong carrying case

A first aid kit for dogs

Prepare a special first aid kit for your dog. The nurse will explain how to use everything. Just like you, your dog sometimes cuts or grazes herself by accident. The kit contains all the things you need to make her feel better on the way to the vet centre.

The nurse holds your dog for the vet

White coat keeps the vet clean

A stethoscope is used to hear a dog's heart beat

Your vet's nurse

The nurse helps your vet. She knows a lot about dogs. When you have any questions about your dog, visit or telephone the nurse at your vet centre.

Your vet

Your vet gives your dog special health checks. If your dog is ill, he will tell you what needs to be done to make her better. He may give you medicine for your dog.

My pet's fact sheet

Try making a fact sheet about your pet dog. Copy the headings on this page, or you can make up your own. Then write in the correct information about your dog.

Floppy ear

Black back

Brown face

White sock

Leave a space to stick in a photograph or draw a picture of your dog. Then label all of your pet's special features.

Name: **Tess**

Birthday: **12th January**

Weight: **3kg (6½ lb)**

Type of food fed: **Complete dry food**

Best game: **Throw and catch**

Vet's name: **Mark Evans**

Nurse's name: **Rebecca Johns**

Vet centre telephone number: **089582 2324**

Medicines and injections

Your dog will be ill if tiny worms live inside her or insects crawl on her coat. To keep them away, the nurse will give you some special medicines for your dog. Germs can also make your dog sick. The vet gives your dog injections every year to help protect her from them.

Index